Insects

Beetles

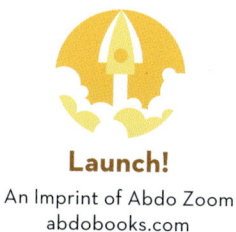

Leo Statts

Launch!
An Imprint of Abdo Zoom
abdobooks.com

abdobooks.com

Published by Abdo Zoom, a division of ABDO, PO Box 398166, Minneapolis, Minnesota 55439. Copyright © 2019 by Abdo Consulting Group, Inc. International copyrights reserved in all countries. No part of this book may be reproduced in any form without written permission from the publisher. Launch!™ is a trademark and logo of Abdo Zoom.

Printed in the United States of America, North Mankato, Minnesota.

092018
012019

THIS BOOK CONTAINS RECYCLED MATERIALS

Photo Credits: Alamy, iStock, Shutterstock

Production Contributors: Kenny Abdo, Jennie Forsberg, Grace Hansen, John Hansen

Design Contributors: Dorothy Toth, Neil Klinepier

Library of Congress Control Number: 2018945592

Publisher's Cataloging-in-Publication Data

Names: Statts, Leo, author.

Title: Beetles / by Leo Statts.

Description: Minneapolis, Minnesota : Abdo Zoom, 2019 | Series: Insects | Includes online resources and index.

Identifiers: ISBN 9781532125065 (lib. bdg.) | ISBN 9781641856515 (pbk) | ISBN 9781532126086 (ebook) | ISBN 9781532126598 (Read-to-me ebook)

Subjects: LCSH: Beetles--Juvenile literature. | Beetles--Behavior--Juvenile literature. | Beetles--Anatomy--Juvenile literature. | Insects--Juvenile literature.

Classification: DDC 595.76--dc23

Table of Contents

Beetles 4

Body 6

Habitat 10

Food 12

Life Cycle 16

Quick Stats 20

Glossary 22

Online Resources 23

Index 24

Beetles

4

There are more than 300,000 known **species** of beetles in the world. But experts believe there could be more than 4 million species!

Body

Most beetles are brown or black. Some beetles can be very colorful.

head · thorax · abdomen

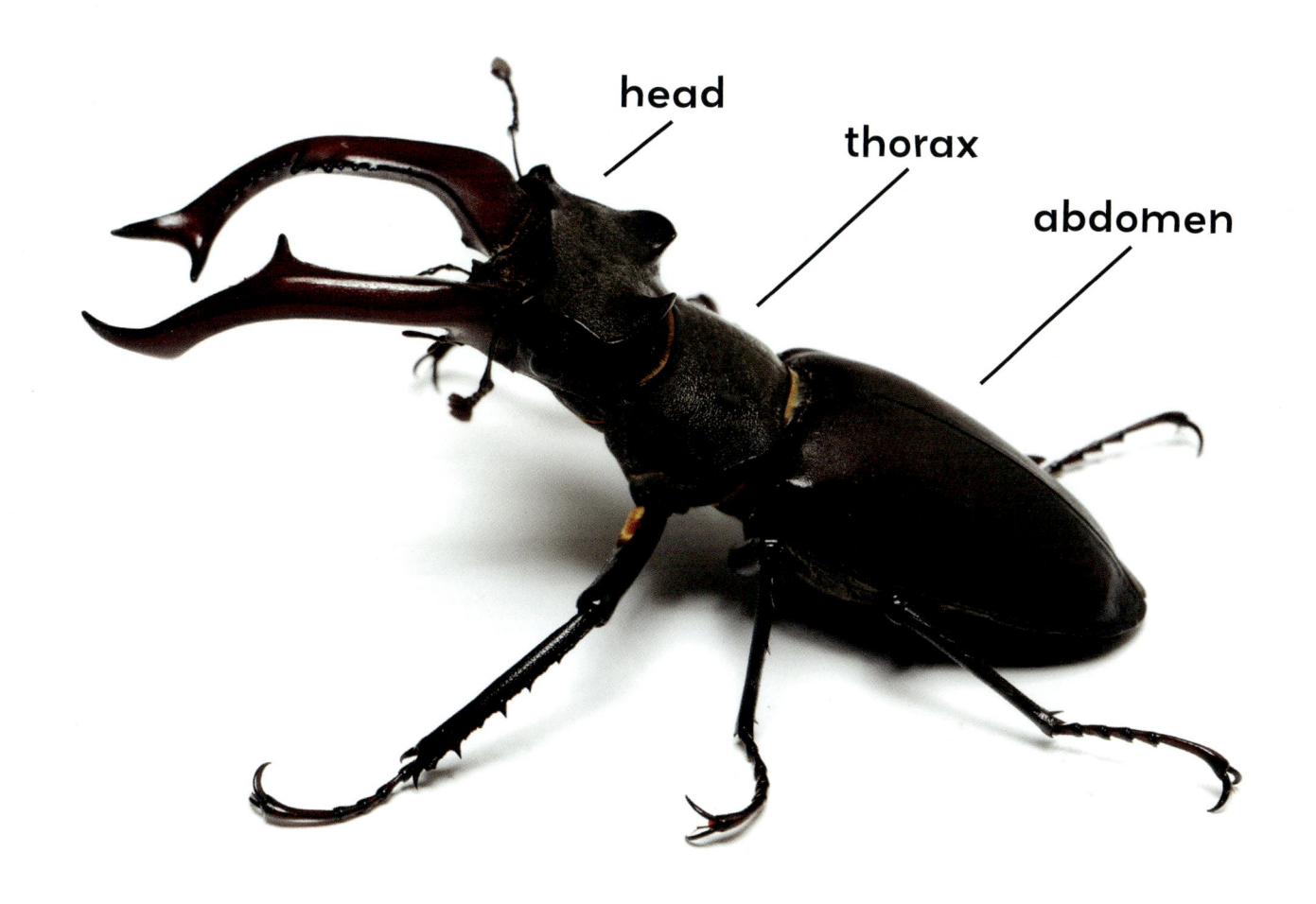

They have three main body parts. They have a head, **thorax**, and **abdomen**.

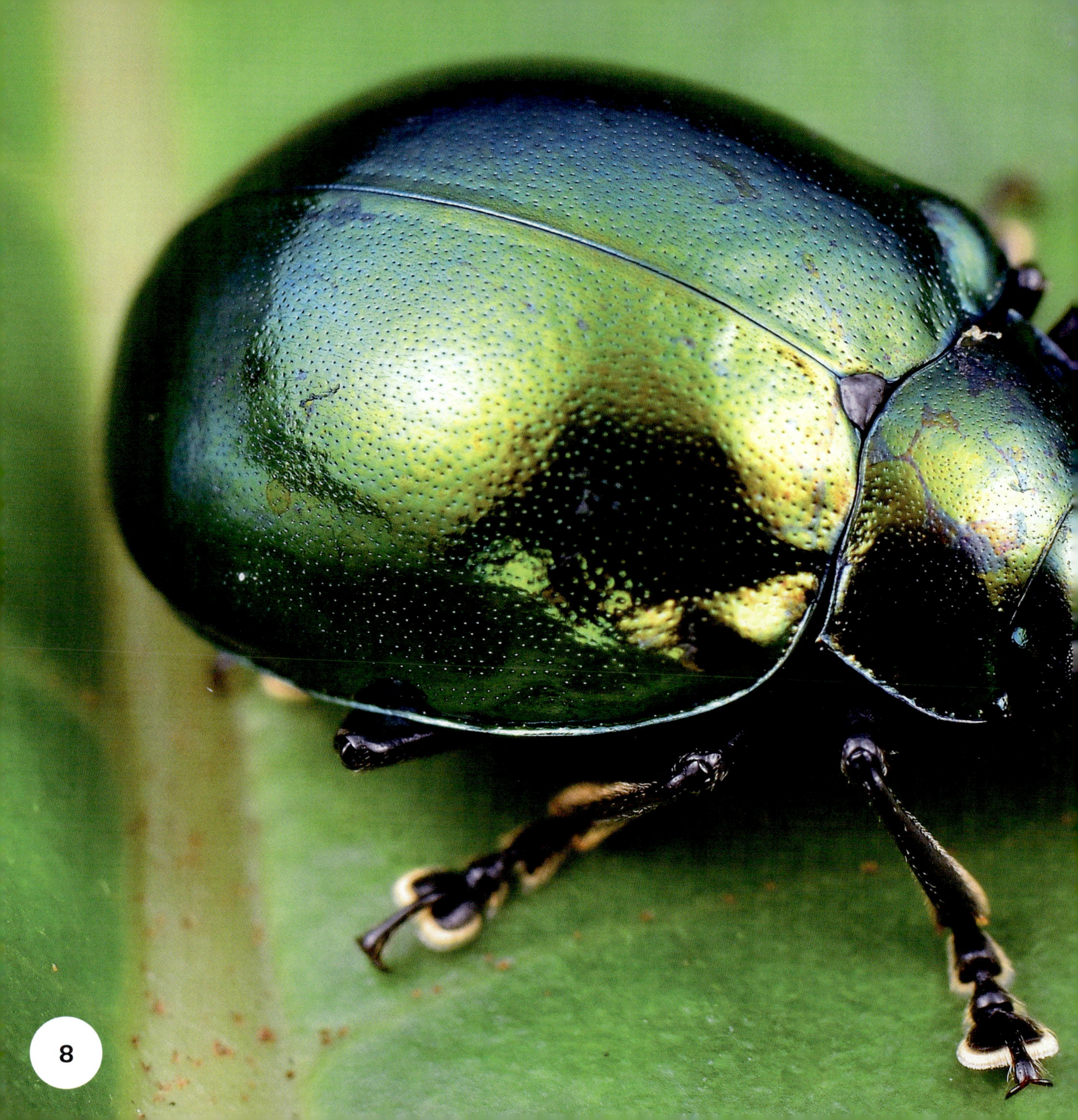

A beetle has a hard shell that covers its body. The shell helps **protect** it.

Habitat

Beetles can be found almost everywhere in the world. They live on land. They also live in **fresh water**.

Food

Beetles can be **carnivores**, **herbivores**, and **omnivores**. It depends on which **species** they are.

Most beetles eat wood, leaves, and fruit.

Some beetles eat small animals or other insects.

Beetles have very strong jaws. This helps them eat their food.

Life Cycle

Female beetles can lay hundreds of eggs.

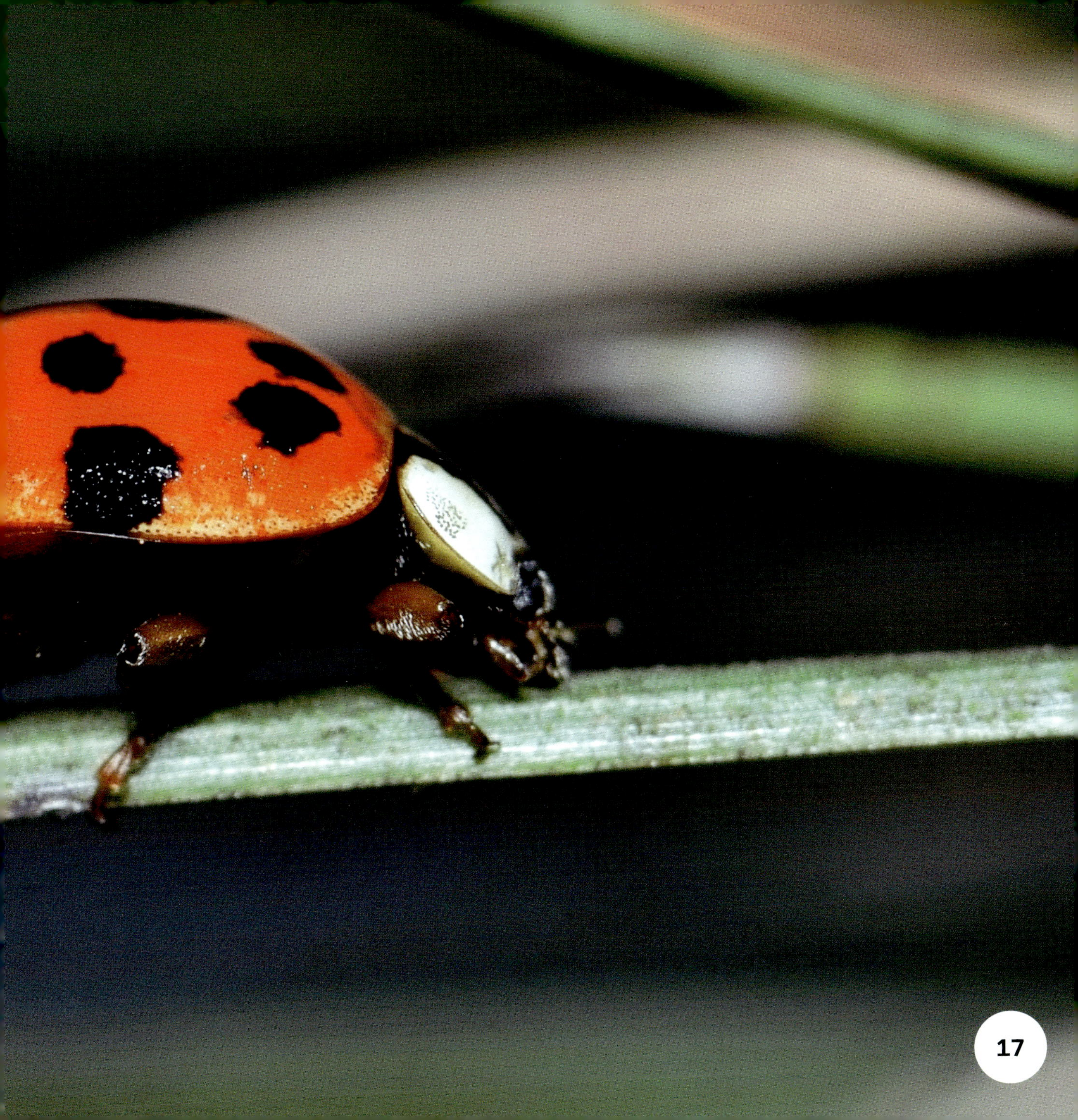

Baby beetles live on their own at first. Most beetles live no longer than one year.

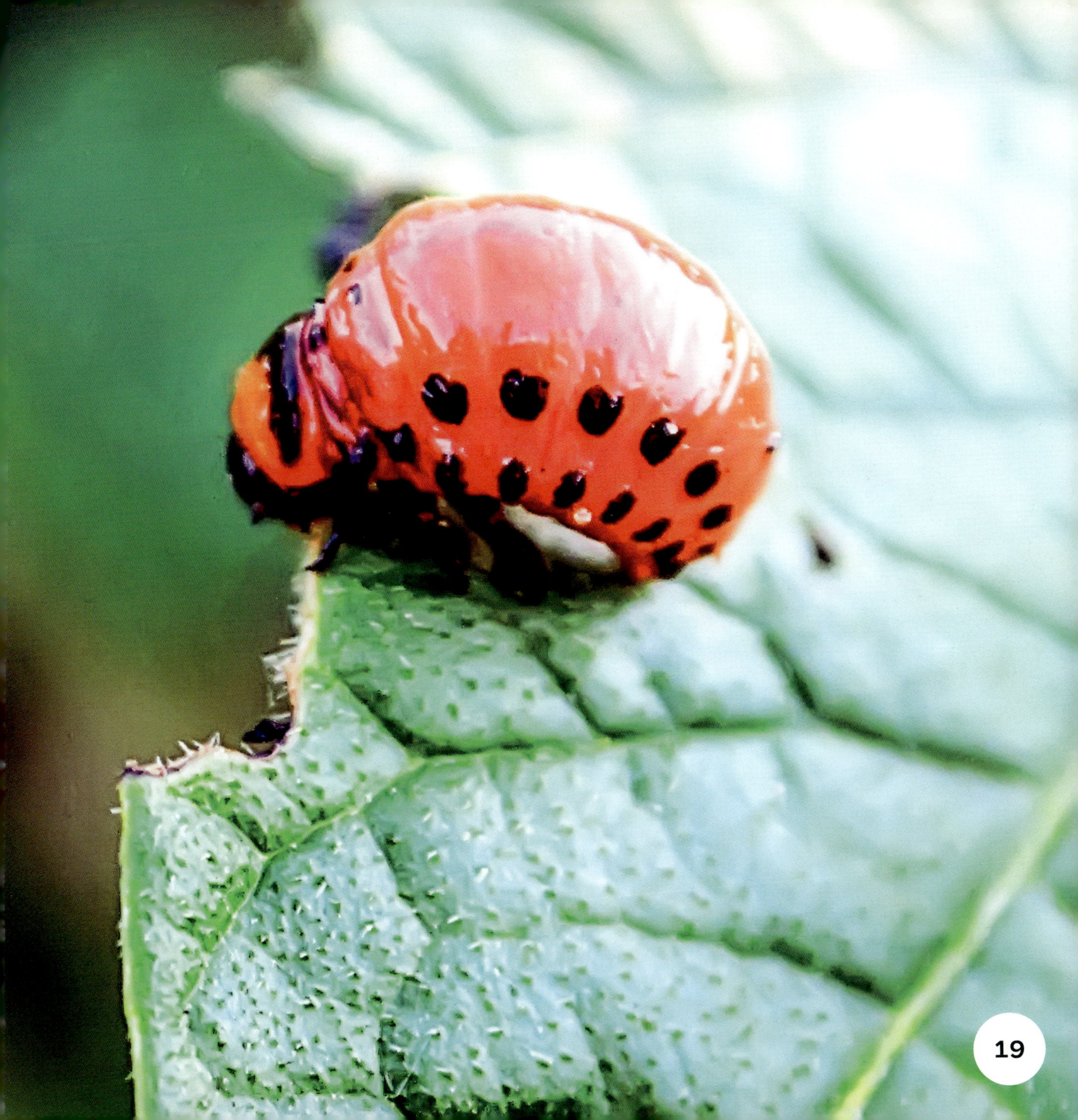

Quick Stats

Average Size – Largest

A long-horned beetle is longer than a baseball.

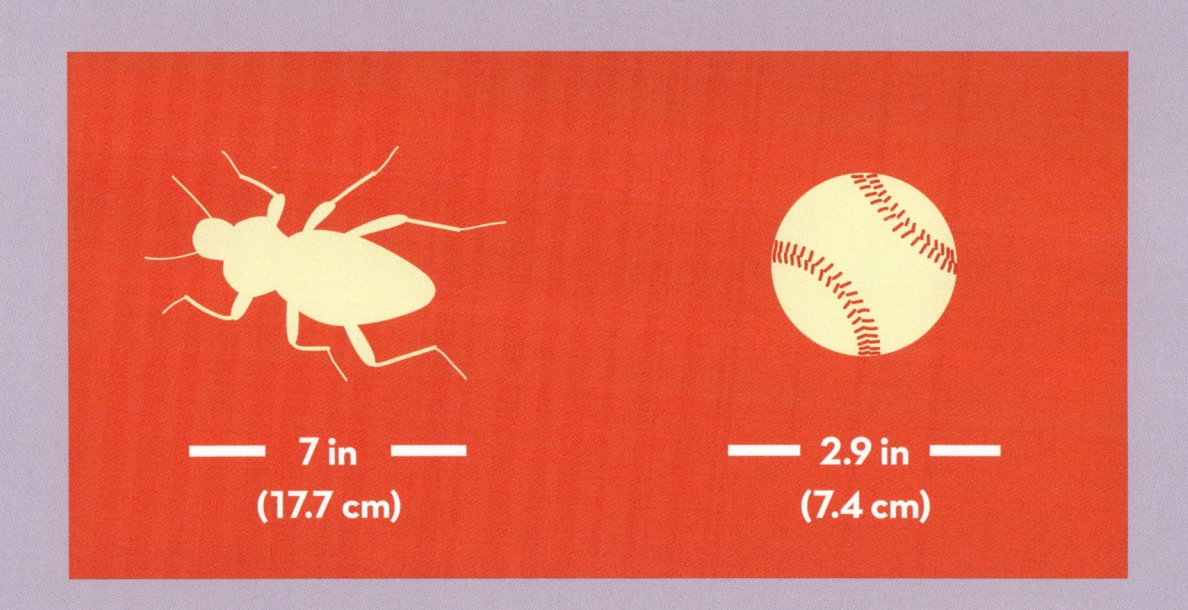

7 in
(17.7 cm)

2.9 in
(7.4 cm)

Quick Stats

Average Size – Smallest

A feather-winged beetle is shorter than a penny.

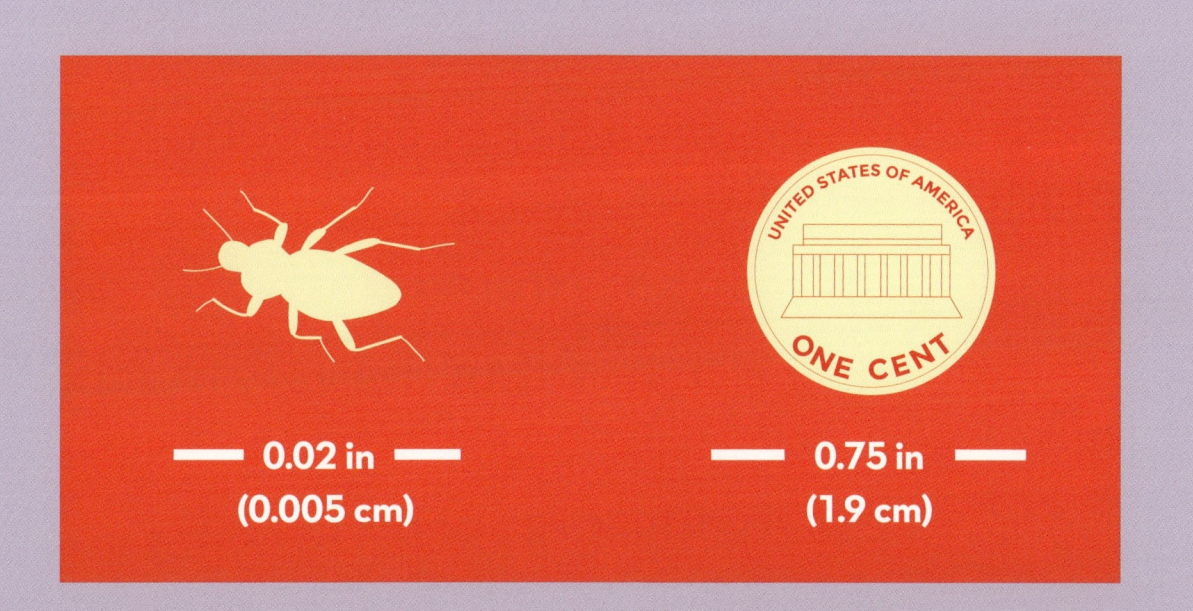

0.02 in
(0.005 cm)

0.75 in
(1.9 cm)

Glossary

abdomen – the back part of an insect's body.

carnivore – an animal that eats flesh.

fresh water – water that does not have salt in it like oceans do.

herbivore – an animal that eats plants.

omnivore – an animal that eats both plants and animals.

protect – to keep safe from harm.

species – living things that are very much alike.

thorax – the middle part of an insect's body.

Online Resources

Booklinks NONFICTION NETWORK
FREE! ONLINE NONFICTION RESOURCES

For more information on beetles, please visit **abdobooklinks.com**

Abdo Zoom DATABASES
BEGINNING ONLINE RESEARCH

Learn even more with the Abdo Zoom Animals database. Visit **abdozoom.com** today!

Index

abdomen 7

babies 18

color 6

eggs 16

food 12, 13, 14, 15

fresh water 11

head 7

jaws 15

land 11

shell 9

species 5

thorax 7